Make her scream

Let it linger longer, hit harder, and be the greatest she's ever experienced.

By

Nicole Smith

TABLE OF CONTENTS

-Enjoy some fantasy in sex

-How to stay harder and longer during sex

-Sex toys 101

-Multiple orgasms

-Do's and Don'ts after sex

-CONCLUSION

INTRODUCTION

Sarah and George had known each other for some time, but had never been very close until one fateful night when they decided to take the plunge and explore each other on a deeper level.

Knowing that they both had a mutual craving for something more than the typical everyday encounter, George revealed his plan to make Sarah scream.

He knew that the key to achieving this was not to simply finish the act as quickly as possible. On the contrary, he told Sarah to prepare for a long night of pleasure as he would make sure to let it linger longer, hit harder, and be the greatest experience she's ever had.

It didn't take long for Sarah to get hot and steamy. Her body uncontrollably shaking from all the sensations that George carefully crafted over the hours-long session. He knew exactly how to touch her in the right places, move her in just the right way, and take her to places she never knew existed.

As Sarah screamed again and again, George made this night one to remember. By the time the session was over, he had given her the greatest experience she's ever had.

Sarah and George's passionate night had found its place in the couple's hearts forever. Whenever they looked back on their time together, they both shared the same sentiment: that George had managed to make her scream louder, longer, and much more intensely than anything either of them had ever felt before. That special night with George was the ultimate testament to how deeply he loved and cared for Sarah, and the only way he knew how to show it was to make her truly feel the pleasure and joy they both deserved.

It was truly the best night for both of them. Since then, George and Sarah have been inseparable, and they both are constantly reminded of that magical night they spent together.

Inside a woman's mind

Sex is a natural and complex part of a female's life. It involves physical, emotional, and psychological aspects that work together to create a powerful and unique experience. On the physical level, a woman's sexual experience can involve a range of sensations, from pleasure to pain. This is largely dominated by hormones – estrogen and progesterone which create different levels of physical arousal. Depending on the individual, her level of hormones may cause her to experience intense pleasure during sex, or alternatively, strong discomfort and even physical pain.

The emotional experience of sex is also unique for each woman. As psychological excitement builds, women can experience a range of feelings ranging from contentment and pleasure to nervousness and fear. This emotional rollercoaster is one of the most fascinating and powerful aspects of a woman's sexual life. Furthermore, her feelings during sex can be greatly influenced by her partner, her relationship to that partner, and her overall level of comfort in the situation.

At the psychological level, a woman's sexual experience can be shaped by the beliefs and values she holds about sex. For example, some women view sex as a meaningful part of an intimate relationship, while others may view it as simply a way to get physical pleasure. Regardless of her viewpoint, these beliefs and values will greatly shape her thoughts, feelings, and behaviors during the experience.

Overall, sex is an experience that involves a complex interplay between hormones, emotions, beliefs, and behaviors. The unique mix of physical, psychological, and emotional elements defines the experience for each woman, and can largely contribute to her overall well-being and happiness.

The values that men and women place on sex are different.

The values that men and women place on sex are different due to numerous psychological and biological factors. From a biological perspective, men and women have different hormones, such as testosterone and estrogen, which can influence the way they value sex. For example, men often have a greater sex drive than women do due to higher levels of testosterone. This can lead to men placing more value on sex as a means of obtaining pleasure and satisfaction. Additionally, cultural attitudes and external messages can influence the way both genders view sex.

For centuries, traditional gender roles have been enforced, instructing men to pursue sex and women to be modest and hesitant about engaging in sexual activity. This idea has been reinforced by movies, TV shows, and music, which often portray men as "players" and women as "innocent" when it comes to sex. As a result, men may feel more entitled to sex and may perceive it as something to be taken rather than given. On the other hand, women may feel obligated to withhold sex until they are in a committed relationship and may see it as something to be shared with a partner.

Though traditional gender roles may be changing, it is important to acknowledge that both men and women are likely to place different values on sex. For example, men may view sex as a stress-reliever and a way to bond with a potential partner. Women, on the other hand, may see sex as an expression of love and intimacy and be less focused on short-term pleasure. Additionally, women may be more likely to engage in risk-assessment and factor in the potential consequences of having sex, such as unwanted pregnancies and sexually transmitted diseases.

It is important to recognize that men and women value sex differently. The biological, cultural, and psychological factors that differentiate genders often affect how they view sex and, thus, the importance they put on it. Therefore, it is pertinent to keep an open dialogue about sex and be aware of the perspectives of both genders. This understanding can help all parties involved in sexual relationships engage in a more positive and respectful way.

The technique of seduction

Seduction is a technique used to attract, interest, and entice another person, typically for the purpose of sexual arousal. This is a process that can require considerable skill and creative effort, and it can be used to bring people closer together in a romantic or intimate way. The goal of seduction is for a person to gain control over the thoughts and desires of another person.

The seduction process involves a range of body language, vocal tones, and other forms of intimate communication strategies. These can be used to indicate sexual interest, break down barriers, appear attractive, and to create an intimate atmosphere. Through this process, seducers attempt to gain the trust and interest of a potential partner without crossing the line into inappropriateness.

Verbal communication is an important factor in seduction. The use of persuasive language and flattery is a key strategy. The intention is to make the target of seduction feel special, important, desired, and respected. This can be accomplished through the use of clever compliments, showing interest in a person's life, and using innuendo to suggest a certain level of intimacy. An important point to remember is that the conversation should remain playful and that the other person should be allowed to exercise control over the conversation.

Non-verbal communication is also an important factor in seduction. Body language such as maintaining eye contact, standing close to the individual, and touching lightly are all seductive behaviors. These types of non-verbal cues show the individual that the seducer is interested, confident, and comfortable. It also sends a message about the seducer's intentions.

In addition to communication, seduction also requires good timing. Recognizing the right moment to escalate the sexual tension is an important skill. Deciding when to move closer, when to touch, or when to light the candles takes careful consideration. Being too aggressive or moving too fast can quickly turn off a potential partner.

Finally, seduction requires the ability to create an atmosphere that is conducive to an intimate encounter. Being in the right physical environment can help set the mood for a romantic encounter. A seductive environment can be created through the use of music, candles, and even certain fragrances.

Seduction is a complex social process that involves a combination of verbal and non-verbal communication. The goal is to gain the trust and interest of a potential partner. This requires skill and creativity in order to indicate sexual interest without appearing too aggressive or intimidating the other person. Seduction also requires careful timing and the ability to create a seductive atmosphere. Through these strategies, seducers can successfully attract, interest, and entice potential partners.

Teasing: caressing the buildup's flames

Teasing is a form of playful communication that can range from lighthearted banter of flirtatious remarks to more intimate forms of sensual stimulation. It often involves a certain sense of playfulness that implies a closeness and mutual understanding between the participants. At its best, teasing can be playful, affectionate, and lighthearted but also possesses a certain amount of risk and stirs up tension. Teasing is a great way to generate an element of anticipation, excitement, and desire. By caressing the buildup's flames, you can heighten a sense of pleasure and heighten the experience.

Teasing allows for beautiful moments of connection and interest. Through teasing, one can not only express their interest in the other person and their attraction, but can also demonstrate their wit and charm. Furthermore, when done in a playful way, teasing can be a way to connect, establish shared humor, and build a sense of rapport and trust. When done correctly, teasing may even lead to greater pleasure and anticipation, setting up for an even more rewarding experience.

Teasing can also be a great way to show one's more playful side, break the ice, and get the other person to open up. It can be an opportunity to share something of a more physical yet still lighthearted nature, to get to know someone on a more personal level. When used as a gentle yet sustained form of arousal, teasing can also be a great way to caress the buildup's flames, keeping the sensations simmering until the point it's close to boiling over.

When teasing, one should always ensure that it remains respectful and consensual to ensure that both parties are comfortable and enjoying the experience. Additionally, in order for teasing to be a successful and pleasurable experience, it requires strong communication and understanding of one another. One should also bear in mind that some people may not be as ready or open as others for teasing and it is important to take those points into account.

To sum it up, teasing is a powerful way to create a playful connection, show one's wit, and create a heightened sense of pleasure and anticipation. By caressing the buildup's flames, one can ensure a steady and enjoyable experience that both parties can enjoy. Ultimately, the goal of teasing is to create an intimate and fully enjoyable experience for both people.It is important, of course, to always practice teasing in a respectful and consensual way to ensure that all needs and boundaries are met. Communication is key to ensure all bases are covered and that all parties are having a pleasant time.

Foreplay technique

Foreplay is often the key to unlocking satisfying and pleasurable physical, emotional, and mental connection and contact between partners during sexual activity. In fact, it is often thought of as even more important than the actual act of sex. Foreplay has the potential to make our sexual experiences more satisfying, enjoyable, and intimate.

First and foremost, it is important to understand what foreplay actually is and what it can do for your relationship. Foreplay is defined as the process of stimulating each other's bodies and minds before the main event. Examples of foreplay can include (but are not limited to) kissing, touching, massaging, teasing, exploring each other's bodies, verbal foreplay, and more.

The goal of foreplay is to increase sexual desire, arousal, and pleasure for both partners. Generally, it intensifies the physical pleasure received during sex and can also increase the emotional connection between partners. Foreplay can also help the physical parts of sex feel better for longer, as the body and mind are more relaxed and ready for the main event.

The key to good foreplay is taking your time. Foreplay should be slow, gentle, and intimate. It is important to pay attention to your partner's body language, reactions, and verbal cues to ensure that your foreplay is enjoyable and satisfying for both of you.

Kissing is often a great way to start foreplay. Beginning by lightly kissing the lips, neck, ears, and other erogenous zones helps to set the mood and build anticipation. Be sure to pay attention to your partner's reactions. This can be a great way to find out what they like and generate ideas for what to do next.

Touching is another important part of foreplay. When touching your partner, start slowly and gradually increase pressure. Focus on lightly caressing one area before moving on to the next. Ask for feedback from your partner to ensure that they are enjoying the experience. Explore every part of your partner's body with your hands, allowing yourself to become familiar with and attentive to their responses.

Massage is also an excellent way to increase both pleasure and relaxation. Lightly massaging the head, neck, arms, and legs can help increase blood flow and sensation throughout the body. Again, make sure to read body language and ask your partner for feedback.

Verbal foreplay can also be exciting and intimate. As you explore each other's bodies, be sure to talk about and describe what you are feeling, as well as what you'd like to do next. Dirty talk and whispering are great ways to increase pleasure as well.

Finally, it is important to remember that foreplay should be fun and enjoyable for both partners. Don't be afraid to mix it up and experiment. Listen to your partner to make sure you are both having a great time and are in sync!

Oral sex: the inside story

Oral sex is a sexual activity that involves the mouth, tongue, teeth, or throat being used to stimulate the genitalia. It is one of the most frequently practiced sexual activities among both, heterosexual and homosexual couples and may involve the use of a range of techniques such as cunnilingus (for female genitalia) or fellatio (for male genitalia).

Cunnilingus is a sexual act in which one person stimulates the genitals of another person with their oral or tongue. It is typically performed on a vulva or vagina and involves licking, probing, and sucking of the external genitalia. It can also include the insertion of the tongue, fingers, toys, or other objects into the vagina. Cunnilingus provides both physical and psychological pleasure and is often seen as an important part of foreplay prior to sexual intercourse.

Unlike other sexual activities, cunnilingus does not involve penetration, so it is generally considered to be less risky in terms of pregnancy and sexually transmitted infections (STIs). The main risks associated with cunnilingus include passing on an infection through the exchange of bodily fluids or contact with the skin, such as herpes or HPV. It's also important to practice safe oral sex and to use condoms or dental dams when performing cunnilingus to reduce the risk of passing on or getting an infection.

Cunnilingus can provide intense pleasure for both partners, due to the many nerve endings that are concentrated in the vulva area. This pleasure can be increased with the use of lubricants, and stimulation of the area can result in intense orgasms. Cunnilingus can increase the arousal of both partners, leading to more pleasurable intercourse. It can also be seen as an expression of intimacy and trust between partners and can be a great way to enhance sexual exploration.

Cunnilingus can be enjoyed by all genders and sexual orientations, and it's important to make sure that any partner engaging in this activity is comfortable and enthusiastic. Communication prior to and during the activity is important to ensure that both partners are comfortable and enjoying the experience.

On the other hand, Fellatio, sometimes referred to as "oral sex," is the practice of stimulating a partner's genitals with one's mouth or tongue. As the name suggests, it is most commonly performed on the penis or vulva, among other areas of the body. Fellatio is an intimate and pleasurable way to engage sexually with a partner, and its popularity and versatility make it a popular choice among same-sex and opposite-sex partners alike.

At its core, fellatio involves stimulating the penis with the mouth or tongue in order to increase pleasure or arousal. It often involves licking, sucking, and caressing the penis and its surrounding areas. Additionally, partners may engage in varying levels of pressure and intensity with their mouths, tongue, and/or hands to elicit different kinds of pleasure and sensation.

Fellatio can be a safe and pleasurable activity with the proper precautions, such as lubrication and correct technique. It is important to consider potential risks before engaging in any form of oral sex, such as the spread of infection, which can occur with any mutual contact.

Lubrication is an important part of fellatio, as it helps to reduce friction and the risk of damage to the sensitive areas of the body. The safest form of lubricant for fellatio is water-based lubricant, which can be found in a variety of forms, including flavored lubricants, which can create an extra pleasant sensation. Lubricant should be reapplied as needed throughout the activity to make sure that both partners remain comfortable and to minimize the risk of sexual transmission of infection or disease.

In addition to lubrication, it is important to consider the approach and technique used when stimulating the body. Every person's body, preferences, and experiences are different, so talk with your partner to determine what kinds of activities and techniques will be most enjoyable for them.

Communication around sexual activity is essential for safety and pleasure, and is especially important for activities like fellatio that involve potentially sensitive areas of the body. Some people may enjoy a more direct approach, while others may prefer a slower, more gentle approach to avoid any discomfort. Talking about what feels good, what doesn't, and when any activity should stop can help create a mutually pleasurable experience.

Overall, fellatio is an intimate and pleasurable experience that can add to a couples' sexual life. By taking the proper precautions and communicating openly and honestly with one another, it can be a safe and enjoyable activity that can be tailored to the individual needs of both partners.

Although oral sex is typically considered to be a safe form of sexual activity, there are some medical risks associated with it. Oral sex is often considered to be more intimate than other forms of sexual intercourse. As physical contact is limited to a mouth and a genital area, it often leads to greater levels of communication and connection between two people than other forms of sexual activities. Also, since direct skin to skin contact isn't included, it can make oral sex a much more comfortable option for sexual expression with a partner.

However, there are a few things to consider when engaging in oral sex. Firstly, there is a risk of transmitting sexually transmitted diseases (STDs). While oral sex can be incredibly enjoyable, it's important to remember that any kind of unprotected sex, including unprotected oral sex, can put you at risk of catching an STD.

It is highly recommended to use a barrier protection such as dental dams or condom when engaging in oral sex. Also, it is important to discuss the issue of sexual history with your partner to ensure that both of you are aware of any potential risks and how they can be minimized.

Another important factor to consider with oral sex is hygiene. Oral sex can cause bacteria and other kinds of microbes to transfer from one person to another which can lead to the transmission of infections and other health problems. It is important to make sure to keep the genital area clean before engaging in oral sex and to avoid contact with any kind of secretions. If needed, one can also use a dental dam or condom in order to keep the genital area free from contact with saliva and other bodily fluids.

It is also important to keep in mind that everyone will have different levels of comfort when it comes to oral sex and it is important to respect these boundaries. Though there is an inherent intimacy to oral sex, it's important to be mindful of your partner's boundaries and to communicate openly about both comfort levels and desires.

A look at the specifics of what attracts women

What attracts women to a potential partner is a complex and nuanced subject, and it's one that can vary from person to person. In general, though, there are a few key areas worth keeping in mind when assessing the qualities that women find attractive.

Physical Appearance: As for physical appearance, men who are more chiseled and muscular can often do well when it comes to women's attraction. Facial features like prominent cheekbones, strong jawline, and unique eyes are also often mentioned in what women find attractive. Having an overall symmetrical physique can be quite attractive as well. However, it's important to remember that physical attractiveness isn't the only factor in play here.

Personality: A sense of humor, intelligence, and confidence are key elements in what women often look for in a man. Being able to carry yourself in a mature and confident manner in all kinds of social situations is one way to appear attractive to the opposite sex. Furthermore, having a good sense of style or knowledge in certain topics can help make you stand out.

Interests: Women find men who have goals and hobbies attractive. If you're passionate about your job, if you're into volunteering or traveling to new places, or if you have a skill you pick up and take seriously, then that is seen as an attractive quality. Showing interest in a woman's hobbies and interests also goes a long way in creating a connection.

Respect: While respect may seem like something basic, it's a huge factor when it comes to a successful relationship. Being respectful of her opinions, ideas, and feelings is important. Demeaning behavior and making her feel as if she is worth less than others is never attractive.

Communication: A big factor in maintaining a strong relationship is the ability to communicate and express one's feelings in a healthy way. Listening to her instead of talking over her, being able to express yourself in a manner that is not patronizing or belittling, and being able to discuss both the good and the bad in your relationship are all key elements here.

Compassion: Showing kindness and understanding towards her and her feelings is a highly attractive characteristic. In areas where you disagree, you should be willing to attack the problem and not place blame on her. Compassion and understanding helps build strong foundations of trust and friendship, which are essential for any relationship.

At the end of the day, it's important to remember that what attracts women to men can vary from person to person. Establishing a connection and having a mutual interest in one another is paramount to creating a successful relationship. The qualities above can be a great guide for developing yourself in an attractive way.

Penetration techniques

A penetration technique is a sexual technique that involves the use of the body, a partner's body, or a sex toy to penetrate a partner's vagina, anus, or mouth. This type of sexual activity can include activities such as fingering, fisting, thrusting, mutual masturbation, and using sex toys. Penetration techniques can be used to increase pleasure, intensity, and satisfaction for all involved.

Fingering is a simple but effective penetration technique. Using the fingers to gently massage and stimulate the clitoris, vagina, or anus can be both pleasurable and very arousing. Going slowly and taking the time to adjust the pressure and focus on specific spots can help build arousal and also help to better understand one's own body and pleasure responses.

Fisting involves the use of one's entire hand to penetrate and explore deeper areas of the body. When done sensually and with careful communication and consent, it can be a very pleasurable and intense experience. Before trying this type of penetration, it is important to take the time to practice using lubricant and to familiarize oneself with the anatomy and sensations that come with fisting.

Thrusting is the most common and traditional penetration technique that has been used throughout history. Starting slow and focusing on gentle rhythms and movements is an important factor in experiencing pleasure. Building up speed and intensity can be a great way to explore different sensations.

Mutual masturbation is a form of penetration that can be shared between two people. This type of activity encourages exploration of each other's bodies while providing direct feedback. Mutual masturbation can be very intimate, and can also help each partner to gain a better understanding of each other's pleasure preferences.

Using sex toys is an excellent way to explore penetration and a wide range of sensations. Using a variety of sizes, shapes, and textures can allow for a variety of different experiences and new ways of stimulating the body. While materials and types of toys can differ, it is always essential to use quality products that can be safely used during penetration.

No matter which penetration technique is used, communication and understanding of the sensations, desires, and boundaries of both partners is absolutely essential for enjoyable and pleasurable experiences. This type of sexual activity should always be consensual to ensure the safety and satisfaction of both involved. It is also important to know and trust that your partner will honor the boundaries in order to experience the most pleasure.

Seven positions for her satisfied pleasure

When it comes to reaching satisfaction in the bedroom, there are seven key positions that should be explored. These positions can help to accommodate a variety of preferences and needs, and can have a positive impact on sexual pleasure. These positions include:

1. **The Cowgirl:** This position allows the woman to be on top and be in full control. She can set the pace of the action and it allows both partners to have a good view of one another.

2. **The Chair:** This is a slightly more sophisticated position, where the man sits in a chair while his partner straddles him in the best position for her pleasure. This allows the woman to control the depth and angle of the thrusts.

3. **The "V" Position:** In this position, the man lies on his back while his partner sits up at a right angle

on top of him. This allows for greater sensitivity in the clitoral area and great G-Spot stimulation.

4. **The Reclining Spoon:** This position is great for slow, intimate sex. It requires the woman to lie on her side, with the man behind her. This position is great for deeper penetration and G-Spot stimulation for the woman.

5. **The Cat:** This position involves the woman on her hands and knees, and the man kneeling over her. This gives a great angle for both partners, and an excellent view of both partners.

6. **Missionary Position:** This position is great for most couples. It allows the man to focus on control and the partner can focus on pleasure. This is great for slow and tender sex.

7. **The Reverse Cowgirl:** This is like the Cowgirl in reverse. The woman lies on her back and her partner sits on top facing away from her. This is an excellent position for G-Spot stimulation for the woman, and

it gives the man a great view. It also allows for great control from the man.

These positions allow partners to experience new and exciting ways to pleasure each other. Every position offers something unique and allows both partners to experience intense pleasure. With a little bit of experimentation, these positions can provide lasting satisfaction and a great way to deepen your relationship.

Orgasm 101

Orgasm can be one of the most pleasurable experiences of life. But for many women, it remains a mysterious, unexplored subject. In an effort to demystify the female orgasm, let's explore the basics of orgasm 101.

The Orgasmic Process

The female orgasm may be a bit harder to define than the male, since its physical signs can vary greatly from woman to woman. Generally, though, five stages comprise the female orgasmic process: excitement, plateau, climax, resolution, and refraction.

Excitement: Also known as arousal, the excitement phase is triggered by sexual stimulation, and is characterized by increased blood flow to the genitals, vaginal lubrication and swelling in the breasts and other erogenous areas. This is the first stage of the sexual response cycle, and usually lasts around 10 minutes.

Plateau: The plateau stage is when arousal and physical tension reaches its highest level. Muscles throughout the body contract and the vagina continues to swell. This stage could last for a few minutes or as little as ten seconds.

Climax: Commonly known as an orgasm or "the big O," climaxing is the third stage of the sexual response cycle. It is typically characterized by a rhythmic contraction of the muscles in the pelvic floor, as well as a sensation of overwhelming pleasure.

Resolution: This is the final physical stage of orgasm, and includes a gradual decrease in heart rate, breathing, and any sexual tension.

Refractory period: This is the post-orgasmic time period, which can last anywhere from minutes to days. During this time, a woman may experience a sense of calm or relaxation, as well as a decrease in sexual appetite.

Factors that Affect Orgasm

When it comes to achieving orgasm, there are many variables at play. Factors such as age, physical condition, medication, lifestyle, and emotional well-being all play a role in how easily or difficult a woman can achieve orgasm.

Another factor that can greatly affect orgasm is the bedroom environment. Creating an environment that is conducive to relaxation and pleasure can include things like dim lighting, pleasant smells, or even music.

Tips for Enhancing Orgasm

Although everyone's experience with orgasm is unique, there are some tips that may help a woman reach orgasm. These may include:

• Communicating with your partner about your needs

• Exploring different fantasies and positions

• Taking time to relax before sex

• Trying new things, such as masturbating

• Experimenting with different types of stimulation

• Learning about your body

• Exploring anal play (with extra lube!)

Orgasm can be an amazing part of a healthy sex life, and with a little know-how, any woman can begin to explore her own pleasure.

Anal sex

Anal sex is an intimate form of sexual activity most often involving the insertion of a penis into the anus of a sexual partner. Anal sex can also include fingering, manual stimulation and the insertion of a sex toy. It is usually practiced between two people who are "comfortable" with the activity and who understand the risks and responsibilities associated with it.

The anus is a delicate area of the body that is susceptible to small tears, which can make it more difficult to engage in anal sex safely. Therefore, it is important to take all necessary steps to ensure that anal sex is practiced in a safe and responsible manner.

First and foremost, it is important to engage in anal sex only with a willing and informed partner who enjoys the activity. It is also important to practice safe sex by using condoms for both partners because unprotected anal sex increases the risk of sexually transmitted infections significantly. In addition, lubrication should be used for a smoother and more pleasurable experience.

Aside from practicing safe sex, it is important for both partners to be aware of, and understand, their body in order to prevent discomfort, pain, or injury. When engaging in anal sex, it is important to go slowly and let your partner be the one who controls the depth and speed of penetration. This will help ensure that both partners enjoy the experience and feel comfortable with the level of penetration.

Finally, it is important to maintain good communication during anal sex. Discussing boundaries, preferences, and expectations before, during, and after engaging in anal sex, is necessary for a safe and pleasurable experience.

Getting intimate

Getting intimate refers to a relationship between two individuals that involves sharing of emotions, thoughts, and desires in a way that is close and trusting. Intimacy is sometimes seen as an act of love, but it can also have other meanings, depending on the people involved.

In the past, getting intimate was seen as something that should only be pursued by couples in committed relationships, such as those in traditional marriages. However, today, it is considered a natural part of relationships for many individuals, regardless of sexual orientation, gender, or marital status. Regardless of its exact meaning, it typically refers to both physical and emotional closeness.

In order to achieve intimacy, it is important to have good communication skills. This means being able to express oneself clearly and being open and honest with the other person. A key part of establishing intimacy is creating a safe and comfortable environment in which to do so. The individuals involved must feel that they can trust the other person and feel safe expressing their feelings and needs, without fear of judgment or ridicule.

It is also important to maintain boundaries while becoming intimate. Both individuals must agree on the limits and be willing to respect the other's boundaries. This means not acting in any way that the other would find uncomfortable or going against their wishes without permission.

In addition to respecting each other's boundaries, it is also important for both individuals to take responsibility for their own expression of intimacy. It is necessary to ensure that one is not pushing the other person too far too quickly and that communication remains respectful at all times.

Showing physical care and affection can be a powerful way of expressing intimacy. This can range from holding hands, cuddling, or embracing.

It is important to note however, that intimacy does not always need to involve physical contact. Simply being respectful and accepting the other person's opinions and feelings is often enough to demonstrate a level of intimacy.

Getting intimate requires a great deal of trust and understanding between two individuals. It is necessary to be compassionate and understand one another, while also being respectful of each other's wishes and boundaries. With this in mind, it is possible to create a relationship that is intimate, nurturing, and respectful.

In all, getting intimate is an individual experience for everyone involved and what works for one may not work for another. Intimacy needs to be negotiated between two people and cannot be forced. It is something that should be developed over time and with mutual trust and respect. While it requires lots of work, the results are often deeply satisfying and rewarding.

Enjoy some fantasy in sex

Fantasy is a powerful weapon to spice up your sex life. It can add a whole new level of arousal and pleasure to your relationship. Fantasy can be used to bring about a deeper connection with your partner, to explore innermost desires, and to enhance your sexual pleasure.

Fantasy can be very liberating. It can allow people to explore desires that they may feel ashamed or embarrassed to express in reality. When engaging in fantasy, remember that no one is judging you. This can create a much safer and more open environment. It can also help people feel more comfortable around each other, and lessen the pressure of performance.

Fantasy doesn't have to be intimidating or a taboo. In fact, many couples find it to be a great way to explore each other's minds and find out what truly turns each other on. It can also be fun! Fantasy can create a sense of playfulness and lightheartedness between partners, while still allowing them to be really honest and creative about what they're interested in.

Playing out a fantasy can be as simple as talking through a scenario, or as elaborate as dressing up and role playing. Having a set of ground rules is important, and will help create a safe and positive experience

Most important thing to keep in mind is that you and your partner should both be comfortable with the fantasy and willing to try different things. Going into a fantasy with an open mind and an open heart will help you both to enjoy and benefit from the experience.

So go ahead - talk to each other, write down your desires, bring in props, make use of your imagination, and let the energy of play take over. Exploring fantasy in the bedroom can take your sex life to a whole new level of pleasure and satisfaction.

Feel free to get creative and explore different ideas alone or with your partner. From building a creative story line together, to using toys or props, to taking an erotic class, there are endless ways to enjoy some fantasy in sex. Be sure to make it fun, and never be afraid to ask for what you want.

How to stay harder and longer during sex

As a man, it can be embarrassing to experience difficulty maintaining an erection during sex. Being unable to stay hard and lasting long enough can lead to disappointment for both partners. However, it's important to understand that having an occasional issue is normal and something that many men experience. That said, there's no reason why you can't take steps to reduce the risks of erectile dysfunction and staying hard and longer during sex.

Erectile dysfunction affects many men of all ages, however men who are over 40 are more likely to be affected. This is why it's important to understand how to keep a hard erection and last longer during sex. Here are some of the top tips that can help you stay hard and last longer in the bedroom:

1. **Get Regular Exercise:** Regular physical activity is important for overall health, and it's particularly beneficial for erectile health. Exercise helps to reduce stress, increase blood flow, and boost testosterone levels — all of which can lead to better erections. In particular, exercises such as jogging and cycling can be beneficial for improving blood flow and stamina.

2.**Eat a Balanced Diet:** Eating a healthy diet is also important for maintaining a strong and long-lasting erection. Eating plenty of nutrient-rich fruits and vegetables, as well as lean proteins, can help provide your body with the nutrients it needs for a healthy sex life. Eating foods high in B-Vitamins, such as leafy greens, can also help to improve erection quality.

3. **Limit Alcohol Intake:** Taking too much alcohol can lead to erectile difficulties. Drinking can reduce the natural production of testosterone and reduce blood flow to the penis. If you suffer from erectile dysfunction, it's best to limit alcohol intake and focus on drinking in moderation.

4. **Manage Stress:** Stress can have a direct impact on our sex lives and it's important to be able to manage stress in order to achieve and maintain an erection. Meditation, yoga, and other forms of exercise can help to reduce stress and improve relaxation. Relaxing music can also help with arousal and satisfaction.

5. **Use ED Drugs:** If lifestyle changes don't produce the desired results, then prescription ED drugs can be used. Medications like Viagra and Cialis are designed to treat erectile dysfunction, and they can provide long-lasting results. Just make sure to

consult your doctor beforehand to make sure that the medications are right for you.

6. **Use Penile Exercises:** Penile exercises, such as kegel exercises, can be helpful for improving the strength and duration of your erections. Limiting the amount of time you take before you ejaculate is important for lasting longer in bed and increasing pleasure. Penile exercises can also help to improve sperm count and boost libido.

By following the above tips, you should be able to drastically reduce the risk of erectile dysfunction and stay harder for longer period during sex. Just remember to take things slowly and ensure that you are in good physical and mental health before engaging in sexual activity. As long as you take good care of yourself, you should be able to enjoy a healthy and fulfilling sex life.

Sex toys 101

Sex toys can be a great way to explore and enhance your pleasure and help you become more comfortable and adventurous when it comes to sex. Whether you're exploring solo or with a partner, sex toys can add a whole new level of excitement and exploration.

To get started with sex toys, here are few tips and facts about sex toys to keep in mind.

1. **Get familiar with different types of toys.** There are a wide range of sex toys available, from vibrators and dildos to cock rings and sex dolls. Each type of toy offers different types of stimulation, so it's important to find one that suits your preferences and needs.

2. **Understand the basics of lube.** Lube is an important part of using sex toys. It helps make insertion or penetration easier and more comfortable, and can also be used to enhance the

sensation. There are different types of lube, so it's important to find one that works best for you.

3. **Read the instructions.** Before using any kind of sex toy, it's important to read the instructions carefully. This will help you know how to use the toy safely and correctly. It's also important to follow the manufacturer's recommendations for cleaning and maintenance to ensure your toy is always as safe and hygienic as possible.

4. **Take it slow.** With any type of sex toy, it's important to start slowly and increase the intensity as you become more comfortable. This will help make sure you don't overstimulate your body.

5. **Remember safety.** When using any type of sex toy, it's important to keep in mind basic safety tips, such as using lube, avoiding sharp edges, and avoiding toys made of porous materials. Non-porous materials such as silicone and glass are the safest and easiest to clean.

6. **Get creative.** Once you've become comfortable with one type of toy, it can be fun to experiment with different toys and combinations. Try using different speeds and intensities or adding something new like a blindfold or handcuffs.

7. **Talk about it.** The key to having a healthy and satisfying sexual relationship is communication, and sex toys are no exception. Talk to your partner about any new toys or activities you're interested in trying. This will help ensure that both of you are on the same page and comfortable with the experience.

Sex toys can be a great way to explore and experience pleasure. They can help you become more comfortable with your body and increase your pleasure. When used responsibly and with care, sex toys can be a fun and safe way to experience sex. Just be sure to follow the instructions and do your research beforehand to make sure you're using them safely and correctly.

Multiple orgasms

The phenomenon of multiple orgasms is one that is both mysterious and intriguing. For many women, the idea of having multiple orgasms in a single session is a foreign concept. However, it is something that is achievable with perseverance, dedication, and the right mindset.

Multiple orgasms are simply the result of having multiple orgasms during sex. This can be achieved by either having multiple orgasms in a row, or by having multiple orgasms of varying intensity. While it may seem daunting, having multiple orgasms is well worth the effort and can be achieved through a variety of different sexual practices.

The first step to having multiple orgasms is to understand your body's arousal cycle. When aroused, your body releases hormones that cause certain parts of your sexual anatomy to become more sensitive. To be able to achieve multiple orgasms, it's important to make sure that you keep your arousal levels elevated and allow yourself to experience the different sensations that come along with it.

When it comes to sexual techniques for achieving multiple orgasms, the most common is an approach referred to as 'edging'. This consists of stimulating yourself just until you're about to reach orgasm, then backing off until the feeling subsides. The second approach to achieving multiple orgasms is to focus on different types of stimulation. This could be through manual stimulation, oral sex, or using sex toys. Try varying the type and intensity of stimulation to figure out what works best for your body.

Finally, it's important to relax and focus on your pleasure before engaging in any of the above approaches. When done correctly, relaxation can help you stay in the moment and allow your body to experience the different sensations associated with multiple orgasms.

Multiple orgasms can be achieved with a bit of practice and experimentation. Finding out what works best for your body and understanding the different approaches to achieving multiple orgasms is key. With the right mindset and effort, you can experience multiple orgasms in no time!

Do's and Don'ts after sex

After sex, there are certain do's and don'ts that you should follow to keep yourself and your partner safe and healthy. Following these simple rules can help make sure that your sexual experiences remain healthy, enjoyable, and emotionally fulfilling.

Do's

1. Always practice safe sex, no matter who you are with. Safe sex includes the use of condoms and water based lubricants during sex. Condoms should also be used anytime two partners are exchanging

bodily fluids during sex. Additionally, if you are engaging in oral sex, use an oral dam or other barrier product to prevent the spread of bodily fluids and STDs.

2. Talk to your partner about the risks involved in having sex with them. Make sure you both know the risks and how best to protect yourselves. Be open and honest about any STDs or infections that either of you may have, so you can both take the necessary precautions to ensure you are both having safe and healthy sex.

3. Even if you are in a monogamous relationship, make sure both you and your partner have been tested for STDs and infections, and are taking the proper steps to protect yourselves.

4. Take the time to talk to your partners about other types of contraception methods that may be practical and effective for the both of you.

5. Make sure to urinate after sex to help flush out any bacteria which may have entered your urethra during sex.

6. Take a moment after sex to connect with your partner and affirm your commitment to each other.

Don'ts

1. Do not engage in sexual activity if either you or your partner is not sober enough to give informed consent.

2. Do not begin or continue any sexual activity without first checking in with your partner to make sure they are on board and comfortable. Forcing someone to have sex with you is never okay.

3. Do not mix alcohol and drugs with sex. Both can lead to poor judgment, clouded judgment, and make it more difficult for partners to communicate and provide true consent.

4. Do not make the assumption that both of you are safe to have unprotected sex. Even if you and your

partner are both monogamous, it is important to get tested for STDs before deciding to forego condoms.

5. Do not automatically assume that one type of contraception is enough to protect you both. Depending on your lifestyle and preferences.

6. Do not forget to consider mental and emotional safety when engaging in sexual activities. Before, during, and after sex, it is important to be mindful about how your partner is feeling and what their comfort level is.

By following these simple do's and don'ts after sex, you and your partner can ensure that your sexual experiences remain enjoyable, healthy, and emotionally fulfilling.

CONCLUSION

Making her scream can be a uniquely powerful and satisfying experience if you do it right. If you want to take it to the next level, let it linger longer, hit harder, and put in the effort to be the greatest she's ever experienced. This way you can create an indelible experience that she will never forget. Take the time to explore her body, find out what drives her wild and pleasure her in ways she has never felt before. Show her that you are committed to making her feel pleasure to the fullest extent. Only then can you make her scream in sheer delight and satisfaction. With a little effort and dedication, you can make her experience so powerful that she will never forget it – and will beg for more.

It is important to remember that everyone likes different sensations and experiences. Make sure to communicate with her and figure out what brings out her loudest cries and greatest pleasure. Once you know the kind of touch she enjoys, make sure to give it back with even more intensity.

If done correctly, making her scream can be a sexually gratifying experience for you both. Enjoy the pleasure of pleasing her and the feeling that comes from knowing that you have given her a night of passion she will never forget. With these tips, you can have any woman screaming out in pleasure.